All About Bears

by Betsy Franco
illustrated by Rosiland Solomon

Printed in the United States of America

ISBN 0-15-317205-3 – All About Bears

Ordering Options
ISBN 0-15-318592-9 (Package of 5)
ISBN 0-15-316985-0 (Grade 1 Package)

2 3 4 5 6 7 8 9 10 179 02 01 00

Look at me. What kind of
bear am I?

I am a grizzly bear. You can
tell by the bump on my back.
Grizzly bears like me live in
North America.

Look at me when I stand on my back legs. How tall do you think I am?

3

I am 8 feet tall! I am
standing up because I hear
a sound. I am looking
for danger.

Sometimes I see people hiking together. What do I do?

5

Most of the time, I run and hide. Sometimes bears will not run away. Never go up to a bear. That would not be wise. Bears are wild.

6

I am hungry. What do I like
to eat?

Grizzly bears eat ripe fruits,
grass, meat, and bark. We
like to dive after fish. I am
always sorry if I do not
catch a big one.

8

It will be winter soon. What
will I do? Where will I go?

In winter, I will go to sleep
inside a den. While I sleep,
I will live on fat from my
body. My cubs will be born
in the den.

These are my baby bears.
They are about the size of
a mouse. When will they go
outside?

Once my cubs can see well,
we can go outside together.
When they are bigger, they
will leave me. They will go
off to live on their own!

Teacher/Family Member ···

Follow That Bear!
Have your child read the sentences and decide which ones tell
something true about grizzly bears. Together, write one more fact
about bears. (Turn the page to find the answers.)

1. Bears eat ripe fruits, grass, meat, and bark.
2. Bears cannot stand on two legs.
3. Baby bears are born in a den.
4. A bear can be 8 feet tall.
5 Bears do not like to eat fish.
6. In winter a bear lives on fat from its body.

 School-Home Connection
Listen as your child reads *All About Bears* to you. Then have your
child tell some things he or she learned about grizzly bears.

Word Count:	229		
Vocabulary Words:	bears	sound	sorry
	while	once	together
Phonic Elements:	Long Vowel: /ī/*i-e*		
	like	time	dive	sometimes
	outside	wise	hide
	inside	size	ripe

···

Answers: Sentences 1, 3, 4, and 6 are true.

Take-Home Books

1
0-15-317205-3
90000 >

9 780153 172052

Monkey Fun

by Elizabeth Field
illustrated by Dave Blanchette

THIS BOOK IS THE PROPERTY OF:

STATE _____

PROVINCE _____

COUNTY _____

PARISH _____

SCHOOL DISTRICT _____

OTHER _____

Book No. _____

Enter information
in spaces
to the left as
instructed

ISSUED TO	Year Used	CONDITION	
		ISSUED	RETURNED

**PUPILS to whom this textbook is issued must not write on any page
or mark any part of it in any way, consumable textbooks excepted.**

1. Teachers should see that the pupil's name is clearly written in ink in the spaces above in every book issued.
2. The following terms should be used in recording the condition of the book: New; Good; Fair; Poor; Bad.